devotional talks on christian commitment

devotional talks on christian commitment

timothy e. moody

 **BAKER BOOK HOUSE**
Grand Rapids, Michigan 49506

Copyright 1986 by
Baker Book House Company

ISBN: 0-8010-6203-9

Printed in the United States of America

To my wife
Alena,
and to our sons,
Caleb and **Luke**—
with love and gratitude

Contents

PART 1 Use Your Mind

Preface

Since the beginning of time humanity has struggled to find meaning in existence. Even our generation, with all of its technological wonders, searches for answers to the basic questions. We want to know why we are here, where we are going, and what it all means.

One of the important things I've learned as a pastor is that folks, in and out of the church, want a religious experience that somehow relates to real life. I think most people don't have any trouble believing in God. The problem comes in understanding where He is in our lives and how He works with us. Once we discover that, then we can begin to live for the right reasons.

The brief essays in this book were written with all of this in mind. They are my own observations of life, and love, and faith, and God. They by no means offer all the answers. If anything, they raise even more questions. Hopefully, they will make you think. But most of all, I trust they will remind you that life is good, that God is with us, and that we can live out our existence with real meaning and worth.

Acknowledgments

A number of people assisted me in preparing this book and I would like to record my gratitude to them.

My thanks to Connie Lee and Bea Eisen for typing the manuscript and for patiently enduring the changes I made along the way. I am also grateful to Frances Wood and Lauda Mae Williamson who carefully read the manuscript and who helped make grammatical corrections.

Finally, very special appreciation is offered to Ramon Haile whose persistent encouragement and support challenged me to put these chapters into print. Without his help this book would still be a stack of scattered pages in a dusty corner of my office.

PART

1 Use
Your
Mind

1

The Adventure of Thinking

Scripture Reading: 1 Kings 19:9–12

In Rudyard Kipling's poem, "The Explorer," a man in frontier days becomes restless in the limited world around him. He feels safe in his isolation, but he also feels the call of something out beyond the mountains. So he leaves his security behind and goes on alone. Half dead, he finally gets through a mountain pass and finds a rich new land. Others eventually follow him and develop the virgin territory. Farms and cities are established. A whole new world opens up for them.

At the end of the poem the explorer reflects on his experiences. He remembers that at the beginning of his journey he called his dreamland a "Never-Never country." And he recalls saying to himself at times, "no sense in going further." But he did press on. He pursued his adventure. He found a new land. He said he was motivated by "His Whisper." It was the inner voice of God that moved this man beyond his isolation to a world of new experiences.

Life always takes on new meaning when we hear "His Whisper." The adventure of Christian faith is responding to God's call to go beyond. There ought to be something of an explorer in all of us. It's doubtful any of us will discover some new geographical location, but we can open up new ideas about God, faith, ministry, and life. There's nothing quite as exciting as the adventure of thinking.

Have you ever stopped to realize that nearly all the tyrants and dictators of the world have tried to keep people from thinking? The ancient pharaohs, the Roman emperors, Lenin, Hitler, Khomeini, and others are among those who have punished people for using their brains.

Jesus was a thinker. He challenged his followers to use their minds. The religious community condemned him for this. They wanted folks to carry around a packaged faith. They preached a religion of answers and facts. Questions and doubts were not allowed. Thinking was not necessary. Just believe. We hear that a lot today, don't we? Jesus would have us ask some questions. He wants us to think about our faith and about God. Don't settle for canned religion. It has a way of spoiling.

Emerson once wrote about a preacher whose theology was so shallow and irrelevant that the great poet was tempted to stop going to church entirely. He spoke of the preacher in these words:

> He had lived in vain. He had not one word suggesting that he had laughed or wept, was married or in love, had been commended, or cheated, or cha-

grined. If he had ever lived and acted, we were none the wiser for it. The capital secret of his profession, namely, to convert life into truth, he had not learned.

Clearly, here was a man who had failed to use his mind.

The adventure of thinking, of expanding our ideas about God and life, deepening our awareness of the truth of Scripture, understanding more fully our own humanity—this is what it means to listen to "His Whisper." The call comes to all of us. New discoveries await our response.

2

Empty Words . . .

Empty Minds . . .

Empty Lives

Scripture Reading: Proverbs 23:6–8

The old Latin expression, "*Vox et praeterea nihil*," which means, "A voice and nothing
more," may be revived in our day. It is plain to
everyone that we are by no means short on voices.
Smooth-talking politicians, articulate news com-
mentators, poetic philosophers, doomsday econ-
omists, polished educators, and melodramatic
preachers all raise their voices with equal passion
asking us to listen to what they have to say. Usually we do. And more often than not it is "*Vox et
praeterea nihil*," a voice and nothing more.

The great need today, however, is not voices. Our
need is more minds. We have an abundance of talking going on. The shortage is in thinking.

Martin Luther King, Jr., the gifted social reformer, once said, "Who doubts that . . . toughness of mind is one of man's greatest needs? Rarely do we find men who willingly engage in hard, solid thinking. There is an almost universal quest for easy answers and half-baked solutions. Nothing pains some people more than having to think."[1]

To be sure, no one knew this better than King. He battled his whole life with people who could speak with loud, impassioned voices, but who never took as much as five minutes to think through their hate and angry prejudice. King was killed, not by one man with a rifle, but by society's ignorance and soft-mindedness. He was killed by all of us who see without thinking, who measure a person's worth by skin color instead of human potential.

John Dryden once lamented in one of his poems:

> But far more numerous was the herd of such
> Who think too little and who talk too much.

Sadly enough, that "herd" is still with us.

Jesus was a thinker. What a marvelous example he gave us of the value of using our minds in the right way. The Gospels tell us of numerous times when he left the company of his disciples and slipped away to pray, to meditate, to think. Jesus wasn't a robot programed by God. Our Lord had a mind of his own. His teachings, so profoundly simple, yet so relevant to the basic issues of life, did not drop out of heaven. Jesus labored over his

---

1. Martin Luther King, Jr., *Strength to Love* (Cleveland, Ohio: Collins World, Fount Books, 1963), p. 10.

ideas and concepts. He thought long and hard about them. It's no wonder they are brilliant, insightful, discerning, and wise.

He once said that what we think is what we are. Of course, he was right. It's not what you say, but what you think, that really determines how you live.

3

The Art of
Drawing Conclusions

Scripture Reading: Matthew 7:1–5

Appearances are not always reliable. What we see is not necessarily what really is. I am reminded of a woman I once read about who became a self-appointed supervisor of morals in her community. One day she accused a certain man in the neighborhood of taking up drinking because "with her own eyes" she had seen his truck in front of a local tavern. The accused man made no defense, but that evening he parked his truck in front of this pious woman's house and left it there all night! She learned in a hurry that appearances can be deceiving.

Several years ago Andy Griffith starred in a movie in which he played the part of a minister. A couple of suspicious and narrow-minded ladies in his church saw him go into a strip joint one afternoon. They were shocked, naturally. Soon rumors were traveling all over the community that the new preacher "had a problem." No one took time to ask why he was there. Everyone just assumed they knew the reason. Come to find out, he had gone there to see about buying an old organ for the church. The movie identified an important truth: appearances are not always dependable.

When I joined the local country club in my community someone sent me an anonymous post card. The typed note informed me that as a minister I shouldn't associate with "that kind of crowd." If the person had signed the card I could have reminded him/her that appearances are not always reliable. Sometimes they don't mean anything at all.

The Boston Strangler, Reverend Jim Jones, even Adolf Hitler all seemed to be fine, hard-working men with great ambitions. As it turned out, in the most hideous ways, appearances were very inaccurate.

In the fourteen years that I have been in the pastorate I have counseled with individuals, who, in the privacy of my office have revealed some of the most surprising and tragic experiences imaginable. Many of them were people I never would have guessed had a problem. In fact, a model deacon in one of my churches went through one of the most pathetic personal struggles I've ever confronted. No one in the congregation had any idea of the kind of raging battle this man and his family were facing.

Every one of us has a history. We all carry our past with us. Someone with a severe drinking problem may appear to be just a wicked old alcoholic. But behind his drunkenness may be some great tragedy in the past. That promiscuous teenage girl who lives only for sexual thrills and gives her body away as if it had no value, may not be just a "cheap little whore." She might, instead, be a frightened child looking for affection and acceptance. That liberal young minister who shocks his congregation with his doubts and far-out ideas, may not be an irreverent and rebellious skeptic. It's possible that he's just trying to be honest in his struggle for truth. That grumpy and unfriendly old store clerk may not be a selfish and insensitive crab. He just might be lonely, or bitter about some past sorrow too great to get over, or frustrated with old age and diminished abilities.

We seldom know everything about everyone. Even our closest friends sometimes have secret heartaches we know nothing about. Because this is so, we must be careful how we interpret appearances.

4

Easy Salvation?

Scripture Reading: Ephesians 2:4–10

Halford Luccock tells in one of his books about a cartoon that once appeared in the *New Yorker* magazine. A neatly dressed woman is standing at the game counter of a large department store. She has just charged something, and the sales clerk is making out the ticket. The woman, while waiting, has glanced at a chessboard spread out on the counter with all the pieces carefully arranged in their proper places. The customer casually asks the clerk, "How do you play it?"

If you've ever played chess you can easily see the humor here. Imagine asking a busy store clerk to tell you in a few minutes how to play chess. This is not a game that can be explained over the counter. Chess is nothing like checkers. It's more like trigonometry! Some people have invested years in the methodical study of this complicated mind game. It isn't something that can be learned while you're signing a sales slip.

A scene similar to this is often repeated by well-meaning people who think they can explain the gospel in a matter of minutes. And so, over the years, we have had preachers and evangelists and other religious experts who have implored us to win people to Christ in the elevator, at the doctor's office, on the golf course, or virtually anywhere, as if committing your life to Christ is as simple and effortless as unwrapping a piece of chewing gum.

I once had an evangelist in my church who thought "soul winning" was as competitive as football. He was determined to increase his statistics while he was at our little country church. One night after the services we went to a local cafe to get something to eat. In front of the building the evangelist stopped a boy on his bicycle, discovered he did not attend church, quoted a Bible verse or two, had him get down on his knees beside his bicycle and repeat a prayer, and presto, the boy was "saved." The evangelist went into the cafe feeling quite proud of himself and praising God, while that poor little boy, looking bewildered and frightened, pedaled off on his bike. I never was able to get him into church.

Christian faith is not something that can be explained while you're waiting for the traffic light to change. It's more complicated than that. It's not a transaction that can be completed in minutes. Like chess, Christian conversion requires thought, study, soul-searching, and commitment. It takes a great deal of time before we fully understand and comprehend the meaning and implications of following Christ. In fact, it takes a lifetime!

5

A Very Modern Sin

Scripture Reading:

1 Corinthians 10:14–22

Idolatry. It's an interesting word. *The American Heritage Dictionary Of The English Language* defines idolatry as, "Blind admiration of or devotion to something or someone."

When we think of idolatry we usually imagine some African village with natives bowing down to a crude rock or chanting around a totem pole. We may even envision a modern-day family worshiping their new boat and skiing equipment as they pass by the church Sunday morning on their way to the lake. Or, we might think of a college student who devotedly polishes, every Saturday afternoon, his economic sports car that gets forty miles to the gallon.

However, idolatry is not isolated to African villages. Nor is it found only among materialistic Americans. It often shows up in unlikely places.

For instance, we seldom think of idolatry in the church but it certainly can be there. In fact, some people worship the church itself. It becomes their salvation. Many have the false notion that belonging to "their" church puts them in everlasting favor with God. And I'm not talking about any particular denomination. All of them are vulnerable to this kind of thinking.

Then there are those in the church who idolize their leaders. The pastor is often the object of their worship. But in doing this they rob him of his humanity. They force him into an imaginary role. They make him indispensable and indestructable. It's true, of course, that some ministers like this. A few even demand it. None deserve it. They are not gods. They are only frail humans susceptible to sin, failure, and tragedy. Like you, they hurt and cry. They have feelings. They are capable of achieving great good for others, but they are also capable of bringing on themselves and their family, shame and dishonor. Church leaders do not have the first or last word on anything. Like you, they are simply pilgrims in the journey of life. They are searching for a meaningful way to live, to know God, and to serve mankind. They need prayer and support. They long for friendship. They want love and acceptance. But most of them have no desire whatsoever to be anyone's idol.

Finally, there is a tendency in the church in nearly every generation to idolize the Bible. This always becomes a dangerous and potentially destructive kind of problem. Throughout the pages of the history of the Christian church are sad accounts of times when innocent people were killed because

15

of differences over the Bible. We must come to understand that this Holy Book is not God. It is not perfect. Only the message within it is divinely inspired. Men wrote the Bible. Men, not gods. Perhaps Luther said it best, "The Bible isn't the Word of God. The Word of God is Jesus Christ and the Bible is the manger in which the baby lies. And there was some straw in the manger, too."

Jesus Christ is the only one worthy to be worshiped. He is to be, so to speak, our idol. Why? Because he, and he alone, meets the one necessary requirement. He is God. And our worship of him is not done in "blind admiration," but rather, it is offered in intelligent faith, genuine gratitude, and honest love.

6

The Destiny of Words

Scripture Reading:

Proverbs 25:11–13

Consider the gift of words.

The prophet Jeremiah once said that the words of God are like fire and a hammer; they can give us warmth or they can break down the barriers we construct and touch us with God's personal message.[1] It was the Old Testament hero Job who said that words rightly used have effective force and power.[2] One of the ancient poets wrote, "Pleasant words are as an honeycomb, sweet to the soul, and health to the bones."[3]

Words. How marvelous they are! They were the first human inventions and are still the most magical things in the world. It has been said that no

1. Jeremiah 23:29.
2. Job 6:25.
3. Proverbs 16:24.

machine man has made, no modern wonder that he has thought up and constructed, is so mysteriously complicated as the mechanism of common speech.

In his delightful little book, *A Touch of Wonder*, Arthur Gordon describes some fascinating moments in his past that have deeply enriched his life. He tells of a summer by the sea in his boyhood days when he met a curious old gentleman who was away from his work trying to regain his health. The man was a teacher. His subject? English. But he was no ordinary teacher. You see, this man loved words, so he called his class "a course in magic," meaning the magic of words.

One day when they were fishing the old gentleman said to the young Gordon, "Words . . . just little black marks on paper. Just sounds in the empty air. But think of the power they have! They can make you laugh or cry, love or hate, fight or run away. They can heal or hurt."[4]

Arthur Gordon never forgot that wise old man. Nor did he forget the kind of magic there is in words. Today he is himself a gifted writer.

Jesus was brilliant in his use of language. He once told his disciples, "The words that I speak unto you, they are spirit, and they are life."[5] One scholar has eloquently described the speech of Jesus by saying, "His words have the jagged edge of the crosscut saw. His figures of speech are crammed with energy. Explosive as hand grenades, they are tossed into the crowds."

4. Arthur Gordon, *A Touch of Wonder* (Old Tappan, New Jersey: Fleming H. Revell Company, Spire Books, 1974), p. 53.
5. John 6:63.

His words still have a shattering effect. Just read them every now and then and see what they do to you.

Our words, too, have great power. As Arthur Gordon's sensitive friend said, "They can heal or hurt." In your relationship with others, be sure you carefully choose and use your words. Speak the ones that help people laugh, and love, and be brave. Use words that heal. It's the only way to show your appreciation for such a wonderful, magical gift.

7

End Times

Scripture Reading: Luke 12:35–40

I once saw a picture of a ball of wax made to look like the earth. At the top of this wax globe and at the bottom were candle wicks burning brightly. Melted wax was mingling together from both ends, covering North and South America, and there was a dishing out effect at top and bottom. There was no caption or title to the picture but the message was pretty obvious. The earth is burning itself out. The world is coming to an end.

This is the kind of picture doomsday prophets like to hang on their walls. Most of them are sincere, well-meaning people. But they want to get the world saved by fear. Like those signs we used to see nailed on trees along the highway, warning "THE END IS NEAR," there is always someone ready to scare us with this end-of-the-world business. Next time you're in a religious book store take a look at the "Eschatology" section (the word means, last things.) You'll be amazed at the number of books written on this subject. The titles alone are unbelievable.

The so-called experts who write about the end of time have got it down to a science. They have their formulas, their predictions, their timetables, and if you don't believe just like they do you're in big trouble. They see some sort of prophetic sign every time the weather changes. Earthquakes and volcanoes really excite them. Many contemporary doomsdayers are convinced the end is now very near. They often claim that the prophetic signs are coming together to indicate that Christ will soon come and end it all. But, of course, this can't happen, they remind us, until a whole lot of folks have been sufficiently tormented and thoroughly punished. We're assured, however, that the "true Christians" will escape all of this and enjoy a grand banquet in heaven while the rest of earth's inhabitants suffer a slow and agonizing death. One would almost think Christians rather like doom, especially when it's impending on someone else.

I believe in the coming of Christ. But my thoughts on the subject are very simple. I don't know how or when it will all happen. I do, however, like what one honest thinker has written about this puzzling issue:

With the second coming of Christ we reach what perhaps to most people seems the greatest phantasmagoria in the whole collection of mumbo-jumbo that goes under the name of Christian doctrine.

For people really suppose that the church teaches that one afternoon—this year, next year, sometime—

Telstar will pick up a picture of Christ, descending from the skies with thousands of angels in train, returning to earth to judge the world.

But I certainly don't believe that. Nor does any intelligent Christian I know.

For the second coming is not something that can be caught by radar or seen on a screen. It's not a truth like that at all.

It stands for the conviction that—however long it takes—Christ must come into everything. There's no part of life from which he can or will be left out.[1]

Jesus did not, for the most part, speak of his return in terms of doom. He spoke of it in terms of hope! And that's how I see it, too. I don't know anything about the details of his coming. But I am convinced that in the end, we shall all be judged by love.

1. John A. T. Robinson, *Endtime*, William Griffin, ed. (New York: The Macmillan Co., Inc., Collier Books, 1979), p. 58.

8

Learning from
the Dictionary

Scripture Reading:

2 Timothy 2:14–19

One day our eldest son, Caleb, asked me the meaning of a certain word. I said we would go to the dictionary to see what the definition was. Caleb became curious. He wanted to know more about this strange book with the meaning of words in it. We spent a long time that evening looking through the dictionary. So now, every so often he asks me to get it down from the book shelf so he can look at some of the pictures. And occasionally, when he can think of a hard word, he'll ask me to read him the definition. Like most young children, he's eager to learn.

The ability to fill our minds with new information is such a wonderful gift. There is so much to learn in life.

Roberto Rossellini, the late Italian film maker, once spoke of the adventure of learning. He reveals a surprising truth in these words:

> I have an immense treasure: my ignorance. For me it is a great joy to overcome it. If I can get others to profit from what I acquire, I have twice as much joy. As long as I go on discovering new things, life will be beautiful, but it will be too short for everything I want to learn.

The idea that our ignorance is "an immense treasure," is a fascinating and challenging thought. When you stop to think about it, the greatest discoveries of life have come to those who struggled with their ignorance, not to those who thought they knew everything. Ben Franklin, Thomas Edison, Henry Ford, George Washington Carver, William Morton, and many others were all men who spoke not of their genius but of their simple desire to explore, to investigate, to learn. They had no idea their inventions and discoveries would change the course of history and affect mankind around the world. They were not trying to be experts, necessarily. They were simply wrestling with their ignorance, hoping to discover some new piece of information, some fresh experience in life that could help man on his earthly journey. Such was the case with Louis Pasteur. One day the great French chemist was looking for a way to keep wine from turning sour. In the process he discovered a way to destroy disease-producing microorganisms. It was his struggle with ignorance that brought us pasteurization.

We need this same kind of honesty in our Christian faith. We do not know all the answers. No one is on such personal terms with God that he can speak for him on every issue in life. There are no Bible experts, really. The scholars who give their entire life to the study and research of Scripture would be the first to admit their ignorance.

It's that way with all of us. We know so little about God, Christ, the Holy Spirit, heaven, hell, miracles, and much more. Our Christian faith confronts us with questions we may never answer; with mysteries we may never solve; with issues we may never fully understand. But this is the adventure of believing. Like a curious young child thumbing through a great complicated book we, too, may stumble on something new in life and in the process stretch our minds and learn.

9

The Benefits
of Experience

Scripture Reading: Job 1:18–22

During the 1981 U.S. Open Tennis Tournament an interesting comment was made by one of the sportscasters. Tracy Austin and Pam Casale were battling it out on the tennis court. Pam was having a difficult time making points even though she was playing quite well. During her struggle one of the broadcasters said, "Casale charges the net and that doesn't work. She slams the lob and that doesn't work. She hits the corner and that doesn't work." Then he said, "Why play?" And after a long pause the other announcer, who was a professional tennis player, said, "She's playing for experience."

Pam Casale is still pretty young. She hasn't been a professional too many years. Though she's a skilled player and a tough competitor, she still has a lot to learn. Naturally she plays each match to win but she also plays for more experience. How else could she improve her game?

The same principle applies to Christian living. For centuries people have asked the followers of God why they believe in him. This has been especially true when the Christian was facing some kind of personal crisis or tragedy.

Do you remember the story of Job? He had lost everything of value—health, family, property. He even lost the respect of his community. In essence his enemies said, "Your God has abandoned you. Your faith is worthless." His friends said, "You've done something bad. There must be some secret sin in your life. God is punishing you for disobedience." His wife said, "Believing in God isn't worth all this humiliation. What possible good has he brought us? Curse him and die." And what did Job do? He kept right on believing. He remained faithful. He didn't give up. Why not? For experience. He had been a pro in this business of faith. The Bible describes him as "a man of blameless and upright life . . . who feared God and set his face against wrongdoing."[1] But even so, he didn't know everything. There was still more to learn about his God. Job was hanging in there to see what his tragedy could teach him.

When Pam Casale was getting beat by Tracy Austin she could have thrown down the tennis ball, kicked her racket across the court, and quit in the middle of the match. She could have given up on tennis and gone home and taken up golf. But she

1. Job 1:1, *The New English Bible*, © The Delegates of the Oxford University Press and the Syndics of the Cambridge University Press, 1961, 1970.

didn't. She played out the match. She eventually lost but, then, winning isn't everything. Learning is.

Job could have given up. He could have been done with God and died with bitterness in his heart. But he didn't. So he, too, learned.

Sometimes life is going to beat up on you and defeat you. Sometimes your faith is going to be weak and you are going to sin and fail. Even though you may get to be a pro in this business of Christian living, you won't always win. But you can always learn. Experience, that's what believing in God is all about.

10

Try Slowing Down

Scripture Reading:

Matthew 11:25–30

It has been said that you and I live in a "pressure-cooker world." Most of us live a hurried, hectic kind of lifestyle. We are plagued by stress, tension, and anxiety. We're all caught up in work and the making of money. We don't know how to relax. We don't understand the meaning of leisure. The poet has put it this way:

> If your nose is close to the grindstone rough,
> And you hold it down there long enough,
> In time you'll say there's no such thing
> As brooks that babble and birds that sing.
> These three will all your world compose:
> Just you, the stone, and your old nose.

Too many of us are still obsessed with the Protestant work ethic. It's the old idea that we demon-

29

strate our worth as a person by the amount of work we produce. The busier, more productive we are, the greater is our sense of personal worth. And this same principle is too often connected with our sense of acceptance by God. We live our Christian faith on the basis that the more we do for God, the more commandments we keep, the more prayers we offer, the more church we attend, the better people we are, then the more God will like us and bless us.

This, however, is a distortion of the gospel Jesus preached. The workaholic, both in life and in religion, misses so many of the real joys of human existence. He's too busy earning a living, or climbing the social ladder, or evangelizing the lost, or helping out at the church that he fails to care for his family, count some stars, smell the flowers, write a love letter, read a good book, or talk to an old friend on the phone. He is so worried about pleasing God or the boss or somebody that he never stops to accept the goodness and gifts he already possesses.

Paul Tournier, the eminent Swiss psychiatrist, illustrates in one of his books how our hang-up with work steals from us so many joys. He writes:

When I was a boy I used to loiter on my way home from school, visiting the village blacksmith in Troines. What poetry was there! I said not a word, and neither did the blacksmith, but there was a mysterious sympathy between us. I was never tired of watching the sheaves of sparks that sprang from the great hammer-beats. Nevertheless I was scolded when I got home: "Why are you so late?

You ought to get your home work done first. You can amuse yourself afterwards." But afterwards, the blacksmith did not cast the same spell![1]

When you stop to think about it, it's frightening to realize how few of us are really capable of enjoying leisure time. Even during vacations we usually exhaust ourselves in endless activity.

Perhaps this is not your problem. If that's the case then I congratulate you. May your tribe increase! If, however, you do have trouble relaxing and enjoying leisure time, then I sympathize with you. But don't let this compulsion of always needing to do something consume you. Fight it. Learn to pause, meditate, and relax. Realize that God accepts you just the way you are. You don't have to earn His love. He gives it freely.

Be creative. Discover your own ways to keep from living with knots in your neck and ulcers in your stomach. And remember the words of Lily Tomlin, "For fast-acting relief, try slowing down."

1. Paul Tournier, *Learn to Grow Old*, trans. Edwin Hudson (New York: Harper & Row; London: SCM Press, 1972), p. 23.

31

PART

2 Open
Your
Heart

11
Defining Success

Scripture Reading: Micah 6:6–8

What is success? How do we know whether or not we have achieved it? How is success measured?

A contemporary author recently wrote, "We must have something to hold up for our children and say, 'This is success, child. Go after it!' "

Perhaps he's right. But the real question is, what do we hold up or point to as being success? Is it the accumulation of money? Probably not. Some people make a fortune by being greedy, dishonest, and manipulative. They may have a huge bank account but we could hardly call them a success.

What if you are in a position of power and prestige? Does that mean you are successful? Maybe. It all depends on how you got your power and influence, and more importantly, how you use it.

A good many people would say that achievement is what success is all about. Making straight A's in school, being captain of the football team, becoming chairman of the board, winning an elected office, owning your own business—this is success. Well, achievement is important. It can be a worthy goal in life. But we all know some very high achievers who have reached the top of whatever they were going after and all they became were arrogant, snooty, aloof, and critical. This is not success.

What about being cultured and "with it"? Couldn't this be considered a qualification for success? Not really. Just because you wear fashionable clothes, read the latest novels, go to the symphony, and watch educational television doesn't necessarily mean anything, except perhaps, that you have good taste.

Well, then, can success be defined? I think so. Nurturing a faith in God, caring about others, learning to be grateful, struggling to be real and honest, these are some of the marks of success. It was, however, Emerson who said it best:

> To laugh often and much; to win the respect of intelligent people and the affection of children; to earn the appreciation of honest critics and endure the betrayal of false friends; to appreciate beauty; to find the best in others; to leave the world a bit better, whether by a healthy child, a garden patch, or a redeemed social condition; to know even one life has breathed easier because you lived. This is to have succeeded.

Who could argue with this beautiful definition of success? Try something, will you? Put these words to the test. Live them out in life and see if they don't work for you.

12

Frightened Birds
or Trusting Children?

Scripture Reading:

Psalm 139:1–2, 17–18

Getting acquainted with God is one of the truly great experiences of life. Some of us were fortunate enough to have been introduced to him in our early years. As very young children we learned that he loves us. Then there came a time when we were older and we decided to make a lifelong commitment to him. We made up our mind to follow his way to the end.

Conversion for most of us is a quiet experience of the heart. There are some, of course, who struggle with this decision. There's nothing quiet about it at all. They run from their moment of truth, trying to hide from God, avoiding his call for fellowship. Somehow they have never discovered that God is not waiting with a whip, handcuffs, and rule book. They do not know that all he wants to do is unlock the chains that bind us. There's no whip or rule book in his hands. He keeps them free of such things so he can easily embrace us when we come to him.

Isn't it a shame that so many people don't know this about God? Why do we keep giving them the idea that God must be pleased with us before He accepts us? Why do some television evangelists make God seem so distant, so angry? Why does the church usually give us the impression that God is more concerned about evil than goodness, more interested in judgment than redemption, more impressed with pious sentiment than honest doubt and questioning?

Perhaps this type of emphasis is why some people run from God and avoid the church. One day Jesus talked to a woman with a rather questionable reputation. We might call her in contemporary language a female hustler. She had been married five times and was living with a man who was not her husband. Jesus didn't call her a woman of the world and tell her how naughty she was. He didn't condemn her and scold her and warn her about the temperature of hell. Instead, he talked to her about "the gift of God." She wasn't familiar with gifts, though. Her philosophy was to steal and lie her way through life. Consequently, she didn't figure there was any way to do that with God so she probably didn't bother to think about him. Jesus, however, told her she didn't have to lie to God. She could be herself. It's that kind of news that somehow makes us want to be truthful. This woman would never again think of God in the same old way. Now she knew he was someone she could get acquainted with.

Kierkegaard, the gifted Danish theologian, once prayed:

Heavenly Father! When the thought of you awakes in our hearts, let it not awake like a frightened bird that thrashes about in fear, but like a peaceful child waking from sleep with a trusting smile.

This is the way we all should come to God. Getting to know him takes a lifetime. But getting introduced to him can happen anytime. It need not be in a struggle of fear and resistance. It can happen as easily as shaking hands with a new friend!

13

A Wise Philosophy

Scripture Reading:

Matthew 25:34–40

A French philosopher once said, "Go very gently today, for everyone you will meet is carrying an almost intolerable burden."

True words indeed. Words we ought to take very seriously. Everywhere we look today we see people in need of understanding and compassion. And I'm not talking just about the destitute and forlorn. Actually no one is excluded. We all need compassion. Even in this day of stylish fashions, health clubs, and expensive cosmetics, our wounds still show. They are clearly seen on our faces—in our attitudes—by our conduct. We can't hide our hurts. Perhaps we shouldn't even try.

Go very gently today, because some near you may have lost a loved one. Their heart is full of pain. All they have left are memories and the hope of some future reunion. This, of course, can provide comfort, but it does not take away the sting of death. Grief can still be felt—and seen.

Go very gently today, because for some couples the privilege of parenting has become a frightening responsibility and an almost intolerable burden. Their teenager has not only grown up, but grown away. Communication is gone. Love is rejected. Values are lost. Drug abuse, casual sex, drunkenness, apathy, disrespect for self and others, and a lack of appreciation for anything worthwhile colors this teen's world and writes his philosophy of life. Mom and Dad wonder where they went wrong. The nights are long for them, and they weep.

Go very gently today, because around you are people grappling with old age. Perhaps their eyesight is poor. Maybe their hearing is gone. Some days their minds are befuddled and life is disoriented. It's no fun when you can't remember or think straight. Diminished abilities cause tension, frustration, depression. How would you feel if you were told you could no longer drive your car? Or stay at home by yourself? What if your only companion was the television? Or a pet cat? Or the children who pass your house on their way to school? A phone call, a love letter, a neighborly visit—these would be so meaningful. But what do you do when the phone is silent, the mailbox is empty, and the neighbors are too busy to speak?

Our Lord walked the streets and villages of his day taking time to demonstrate compassion and understanding. He felt the hurts of people. He could see it in their faces. Sometimes he touched. Often he spoke words of encouragement. Always he took time to care, to listen, to be patient, and to love. His compassion brought healing and hope. Your acts of compassion can do the same. Decide to go very gently today.

14

Weddings—
Cause for Celebration

Scripture Reading: John 2:1–10

I like weddings. They're exciting. Sometimes, though, they are unpredictable. Once a bride fainted during the ceremony. And one time there was a long pause at the beginning of a wedding I was performing. The little flower girl, who had done so beautifully during rehearsal, wouldn't come down the aisle. She finally dropped her basket and ran off crying. She was terrified! I told her afterward that it was okay and that I still get scared too. She smiled, but not very much.

As a minister, I find there is something warm, touching, and personal about joining two people in marriage. I feel hopeful at weddings. I like the atmosphere of love I nearly always sense among the family, between friends, and from the bride and groom. I feel close to God at weddings. It's not sentiment I feel. It's him. It's his presence. I see him in the candles with their flames burning brightly. I hear him in the music. He is reflected in the smiles of friends watching with anticipation, in the tears of parents yielding their son or daughter to adulthood and independence, in the faces of the bride and groom exchanging their vows and promising to love each other till death forces them apart.

The wedding ceremony is, of course, only a small part of the marriage experience. After the rice is thrown comes a lot of hard work, commitment, sacrifice, patience, and care if the marriage is to grow and develop. One of the old Puritan preachers once gave this advice about a man getting married, "First, he must choose his love, and then he must love his choice." That's pretty good counsel. The wedding ceremony may be performed in a kind of enchanting mist, but living together as husband and wife, day in and day out, may not be all that romantic. There's nothing like the realism of dirty socks on the floor or a bathroom cluttered with makeup, curling iron and blow-dryer, to make a couple remember their wedding vows.

But even with all the tears, fears, struggles, frustrations, irritations, and aggravations, marriage is still a great adventure. Maybe married couples are trying harder these days. I hope so. It's obvious that divorce, though sometimes unavoidable, creates monstrous problems. We need marriage. One contemporary woman has said that "human beings, male and female, still seem to need a mate, a bed to share, someone to raise children with, someone to love even if you have a cold, lost your job, or had a nightmare; and the world is so full of nightmares it's good to have someone to wake with, to hold on to, to remember last year with and make plans for next."[1]

Jesus turned ordinary water into delicious wine at a wedding. He wasn't trying to improve the refreshments. What he was doing was saying that this can happen in marriage. Two common lives can come together in love and faith and become something beautiful. As the wine blessed the people so can a good marriage bless us all. I think it's the hope of that happening that makes me enjoy weddings so much.

1. Anne Roiphe, "Marriage," *Vogue*, 165:103 (January 1975).

15

A New Emphasis
for Christians

Scripture Reading: John 10:7–10

Lately I have been caught up with the realization of how beautiful life is and how we ought to see it as a marvelous gift.

One of the real tragedies of some churches in our day is the overemphasis they place on the bad in life, the evil and sin of society. Too many ministers today enter the pulpit with a frown. Their message is always one of judgment. The world is doomed. The end is near. Little is said about the sheer beauty of so much of life. Such stress on the negative side of things has a way of producing what Gaston Foote referred to as "sour saints." Dr. Foote was for many years the Senior Minister of the First Methodist Church in Ft. Worth, Texas. He once commented on these "sour saints" by saying:

I have met my quota of sour saints, but it seems their sour dispositions obliterated their sainthood. I know mothers who worried so much over their children that they transformed motherhood to smotherhood. I know teetotalers so obnoxious as to drive us to drink, pacifists who make us want to fight, and superpatriots who are living arguments for betrayal. When righteousness becomes self-righteousness the results are calamitous.

All of this reminds me of something a wise old preacher said to a group of pious church members who wanted him to preach about the wrath and vengeance of God. The old pastor said, "Your God is my devil."

Those who disagree with this are quick to contend that the Bible presents a pretty negative picture regarding human life. This is why we must emphasize the bad. I find this argument very disturbing and basically untrue. The Scriptures provide a marvelous balance concerning the reality of good and evil in both people and our world. I for one am not ready or willing to admit that everything belongs to the devil and that God is doing His best to win everything and everyone back. That is giving too much power to evil. Humankind and the world has never belonged to a devil, nor will it.

The gifted writer, John Ruskin, once said, "All real joy and power of progress depend on finding something to reverence, and all the baseness and misery of humanity begin in a habit of disdain."

"Something to reverence"—this is the key to a life that is happy and meaningful. God, of course, is the beginning point for our reverence. From him we move out to respect and admire his creation, including all people and the world we live in.

Jesus declared that life is good. He took time to observe the beauty around him in nature, in children, in the skill and crafts of men, and in everyday experiences of life. As his followers, should we do any less?

16

How to Use a Compass
and Tape Measure

Scripture Reading: Luke 18:9–14

The gifted American poet and writer, Oliver Wendell Holmes, loved to walk in the deep woods near his home in Cambridge. He always carried two things with him: a measuring tape and a compass. He loved large trees, and on his walks would stop and measure their circumference. He carried the compass to make sure he didn't get lost.

That is an attractive picture of a grand old man. It is also an imaginative but true symbol of two things that Christian faith gives to all who follow Christ, measurement and direction.

Being a Christian is not just a label we wear. Faith in God is not just an expression. There really is something to this experience of Christian living.

For one thing, our commitment to Christ helps us determine the basic magnitude of things. He is

49

our "measuring tape," so to speak. We know by his life what is important, what matters most. We discover from his teachings the issues in life that are truly great and those that are really quite small. We learn from him the reality of God. He teaches us that man is a child of God and has value in his sight, and that this is true of all men regardless of race, color, or class. He demonstrates the reality of moral laws binding on all people and all nations. He demands that we stand for human rights and fundamental freedoms. He lived for moral decency, for the sense of personal responsibility, for good will in every human relationship, for mercy, compassion, the spirit of forgiveness and reconciliation, and he challenged us to do the same.

But there is something else. Christ provides direction in life. He is our "compass." And in the process of following him he helps us take the most momentous journey in life, the journey from "I" to "You," from selfishness to mature altruism.

If there was one particular thing that Jesus sternly condemned, it was the excessive and wrong use of the pronoun "I." Nothing is more damning than an uncontrolled ego. Jesus made this clear in his story about the man who prayed publicly on the steps of the temple (Luke 18:9–14). This Pharisee congratulated himself on his fine prayer and his religious devotion and in the process used the word "I" five times. Like a childish character in a nursery rhyme, he was saying, "What a good boy am I!" Then there was the fellow who was so wealthy and so prosperous that he didn't know what to do with all his possessions (Luke 12:13–21). Instead of sharing them with others he decided to build bigger and better places to store them. Gloating over his riches he used the words "*I*" and "*my*" thirteen times! But God called him a "fool" because he was about to die and he had made no preparations for that. The man had been too busy with himself to even realize his own mortality.

Christ offers us a broader path to follow. He gives us direction, which if we follow, will lead us away from ourselves and on out to care and concern for others.

Measurement and direction, these are part of the resources God offers to all who give him their faith. And when life has concluded, what we have valued as important and how far we have gone beyond ourselves, that will be what really mattered.

17

A Miracle
Is Not the Answer

Scripture Reading: Mark 8:34–38

The statistics on those who are overweight in this country are staggering. Millions of folks struggle to keep their waistline trim. But what's really incredible are the kinds of gimmicks customers will pay for to get rid of their fat. For example, you can actually buy special eyeglasses that are supposed to kill your appetite. There's a certain bath oil which the manufacturer promises will dissolve fat cells. Then there's all those diet candies and cookies that you can purchase at the grocery store. The idea is you can lose weight and at the same time have a tasty little snack. Or, as I saw not too long ago on television, you can travel to a beautiful resort in sunny Florida, and in the midst of swaying palm trees eat fresh fruit by the pool side and listen to entertaining lectures on weight control.

It seems that almost any scheme can be sold if the sponsors can assure the plump consumers that they can trim down without pain, exertion, sweat, or self-denial. In fact, a spokesman for the Better Business Bureau recently said that today's miracle cures for fat are so popular because there are so many desperate consumers who want to believe there is an easy way to get rid of their weight problem.

Unfortunately this is an attitude that often carries over into other areas in our lives—such as our religious commitments. We are tempted these days to try to have a satisfying and enriching Christian life without any effort, pain, or self-denial. And there's plenty of religious experts around who are more than happy to offer us just what we want. We're told that if we'll just "come to Jesus" we can have healing, riches, success, fun, happiness, and—oh, yes, victory, by all means, victory. But this approach cheapens the Christian experience and turns it into some sort of carnival of thrills or makes it out to be a kind of football game where believers gather in the end zone shouting "We won! We won!"

When I read the New Testament I can't get away from the idea that Christ's followers are to carry their own cross. What I think Jesus meant is that we are to humbly, obediently, in a spirit of self-denial, suffer with the world in its pain and sin and failure. We are to love unconditionally—and that's not easy! And neither is working for peace, or learning to forgive, or caring for the hungry.

The church today can offer miracle cures for sin or whatever. But most of them will be about as effective as trying to curb your appetite by putting on a pair of magic eyeglasses.

There's a better way for Christians, but it won't be easy. It's the way of commitment, sacrifice, and compassion. But like a rigorous diet program, it will ultimately be worthwhile.

18

Why Are We Here?

Scripture Reading: Psalm 8

One of the recurring questions that rises up from the deepest part of all of us is the one that asks why we are here.

Children, of course, are not too interested in this issue. They're having so much fun just living that they don't worry about a reason for being. Teenagers, however, are different. They struggle with it. Adolescence is such an awkward and confusing time, and much of the conflict comes from this question, Why am I here? Adults wonder about it too. Especially does the question surface when we are in the middle-age period. Suddenly half of our life has flown by and we wonder where the rest of it will take us. We ponder what we have achieved and what's left, and we think, What in the world is it all about? Senior adults raise the question, also. They reflect back on a lifetime of living. They contemplate death, not in a morbid way but realistically, realizing it's not that far off. In a meditative mood they may ask themselves, Have I accomplished what I was here to do?

Ah, yes, this business of wondering about a reason for being is a profound and universal struggle. Sooner or later we all ask, What am I doing here?

That wonderfully gifted Catholic, the late Archbishop Fulton J. Sheen, once said something that helps us understand our existence. In his book, *The Electronic Christian*, he gives us a clue as to why we are here. He writes:

> Why . . . did God create a world? God created the world for something like the same reason that we find it hard to keep a secret! Good things are hard to keep. The rose is good and tells its secret in perfume. The sun is good and tells its secret in light and heat. Man is good and tells the secret of his goodness in the language of thought . . . God could not keep, as it were, the secret of His Love, and the telling of it was Creation.[1]

We are not here because God was lonely and needed companionship. He did not create us out of boredom. We are not the objects of his amusement. He was not some cosmic scientist who one day, as a result of laboratory experiments, produced us.

The truth is, our reason for being is surrounded in mystery. However, there have been moments of revelation. History, the Bible, and yes, Jesus, have all given us clues as to why we are here. It has

1. Fulton J. Sheen, *The Electronic Christian* (New York: The Macmillan Co., Inc., 1979), pp. 4–5.

something to do with God sharing himself with us—letting us in on his joy, his love, his hope. We are here for him and for each other. And if we can just spend part of our time on earth understanding that, and acting on it, then our living will not have been in vain.

19

Forgiveness
Has a Price Tag

Scripture Reference:

Matthew 6:9–15

Heinrich Heine, the German poet, was never known for his sympathies. He was not a man of great compassion. Life had somehow mistreated him in ways he could not forget. Certain people had apparently offended and wronged him in ways he could not forgive. He became sullen, cynical, bitter.

In a moment of satirical honesty, Heine reveals himself in these words:

My nature is the most peaceful in the world. All I ask is a simple cottage, a decent bed, good food, some flowers in front of my window, and a few trees beside my door. Then, if God wanted to make me completely happy, he would let me enjoy the spectacle of six or seven of my enemies dangling from those trees. I would forgive them all the wrongs they have done me—forgive them from the bottom of my heart, for we must forgive our enemies. But not until they are hanged!

This sounds almost humorous until we realize how commonly this spirit prevails in our world. We all find it difficult to forgive those who have hurt us in some way or another. I once had an older pastor whom I greatly admired tell me how his two sons had been mocked in college for their faith. He blamed some professors who had been particularly hard on the boys. With rage in his eyes the pastor said to me, "I tell you, Tim, I'll never forgive those men!" I could understand his hurt, but "never" is a long time. The man is now retired from the pastorate. Perhaps it's best. He's still a very bitter, angry man.

Forgiveness is no easy task. Do you remember what Jesus said in the story of the man sick with palsy? He asked the scribes, "Which is easier, to say, 'Your sins are forgiven'; or to say, 'Rise and walk?' " (Matt. 9:5, NASB). What Jesus implied was, it's always easier to meet some human need than it is to forgive someone.

My older pastor friend, overwhelmed these many years with his hate, must know how hard it is to forgive. As a minister he can preach sermons and save souls, but that's no way out. He can visit the sick and humbly help others, but that's no way out either. There's only one way—he must confront his pain, confess his hate, and seek forgiveness. Then *he* must forgive. This is no easy process. Forgiveness never is.

Nothing reminds us of this more than the cross of Christ. It shows us it was not easy even for God to forgive. The cost was tremendous! And it will cost you and me, too. Unless we're willing to pay the price of forgiveness, we'll never rise higher than Heinrich Heine, who could forgive his enemies only if they were punished.

20

Today Is All We Have!

Scripture Reading:

Ephesians 5:13–17

An ancient proverb has wisely warned: "Time is a file that wears the days away and makes no noise."

Time has a way of slipping up on us until one day we look into the mirror and see at last our aging face and body. The gray and thinning hair, the wrinkles carved by worry, the shoulders stooped by the burdens of life, and the excess weight from overindulgence—these are reminders that life is passing swiftly by. They are not ugly features. We must not be ashamed by them. They are simply part of the marking of time.

It was Shakespeare in one of his sonnets who said: "O! call back yesterday, bid time return." But time doesn't come back. Instead, it moves on without the slightest pause in its pace.

A contemporary poet has expressed the value of time by stressing the importance of even the moment.

He writes:

> Halfway through shaving, it came—
> the word for a poem.
> I should have scribbled it
> on the mirror with a soapy finger,
> or shouted it to my wife in the kitchen,
> or muttered it to myself till it ran
> in my head like a tune.
>
> But now it's gone with the whiskers
> down the drain. Gone forever,
> like the girls I never kissed,
> and the places I never visited—
> the lost lives I never lived.[1]

Here is a profound reminder that time in all its lengths—years, months, weeks, days, hours, minutes, seconds—is precious beyond measure. A good intention never acted out becomes lost forever. An idea mulled over but never expressed fades into oblivion. A wish locked up in secret becomes absorbed in the silence and never enters reality.

Jesus emphasized the importance of now. He refused to be pushed through the crowds by his schedule-conscious disciples. Instead, he stopped to embrace children, hold the hands of the sick and feeble, touch the faces of the lonely, and speak hope to the guilty and forsaken. He did this because he

1. Stephen Dunnding, Edward Lueders, and Hugh Smith, comps., *Reflections On a Gift of Watermelon Pickle . . . And Other Modern Verse* (Glenview, Illinois: Scott, Foresman and Company, 1966), p. 18.

loved, and so that we, looking on, might learn how to use our time.

The hands on the clock are always moving. Today, write a letter, make a visit, use the phone, speak to a neighbor, smile at a child, hold a loved one close. Today, let's show someone we care. After all, today is all the time we have.

PART

3 Look
Into
Your
Soul

21

An Idea Too Big
for the Mind

Scripture Reading: John 14:6–11

There was once a man who was searching for a deeper understanding of God. One night he had a dream. Here is what he saw:

> I saw a friend standing on a hilltop, and I, and a great host of friends, were crowded around waiting eagerly for what he had to say. We could see his lips framing the word, but no sound came. We tried to help him by calling out the word his lips were forming; but we couldn't; and that word, was God.

How do you explain God to others, to yourself? Is he a cosmic force? Is he a kind old grandfather? Is he a stern judge? Is he simply an idea, a hope, a mystery, or what?

I think God knew the world would have a difficult time conceptualizing who he was and what he was like. Plato once said the human mind is not big enough to comprehend the vast idea of God. Surely God anticipated that.

We know now he tried to reveal himself to humankind long before the coming of Jesus. But we did not understand. God disclosed himself in nature, but we misunderstood, and thought of him only when lightning struck.

He revealed himself through the prophets, but again, we refused to listen and so failed to get the message.

For a long time the idea of God was there but that was not enough. It is only when an idea takes shape and form that it becomes powerful. For example, unselfishness is a wonderful idea, but we don't fall in love with unselfishness. Instead, we fall in love with an unselfish *person.*

The idea of God, then, was not adequate. The idea that he loved humankind and sought fellowship with them needed to be demonstrated. And so, the idea of God was personalized in the character of Jesus Christ.

Harry Emerson Fosdick once stated that it took the followers of Jesus a while to understand what his coming really meant and why he was here.

Fosdick sums up what happened:

> . . .at first they may have said, God sent him. After a while that sounded too cold, as though God were a bow and Jesus the arrow. That would not do. God did more than send him. So . . . they went on to say, God is with him. That went deeper. Yet, as their experience with him progressed, it was not

adequate. God was more than with him. So at last we catch the reverent accents of a new conviction, God came in him.[1]

Jesus does not show us all of God. But he has shown us enough. Now we know him to be full of love and grace and acceptance. This is enough for a commitment of faith, and a desire to go his way in life and death.

1. Quoted by Merril R. Abbey, *The Shape of the Gospel: Interpreting The Bible Through the Christian Year* (Nashville: Abingdon Press, 1970), pp. 26–27.

22

Temporary Markings

Scripture Reading:

1 Timothy 4:9–16

Arthur Mayer, in his book *Merely Colossal*, tells of a strange experience in connection with a publicity stunt for a movie he was promoting. He hired a stunt man who could stay buried for twenty-four hours without suffocating. For several days the newspapers carried stories about Mayer burying a man alive. Finally, a day was set and the man was placed in the ground. The exact spot was carefully marked with lime so it could easily be found. But during the night a heavy rain washed away all the markings. Next day, they couldn't tell where the man was buried. It took thirty men digging frantically all over the area before the man was found.

This experience reminds us that we all sometimes lose track of someone or something valuable. Most of us clearly marked those important events in life that meant so much to us at the time. Our wedding day, for example, was an event in our personal history that we planned to always remember. But today when we can get a "quick" divorce for as little as $68.00 it makes me think that maybe the markings around the marriage commitment are no longer so easily visible.

For most of us there was also a time when we possessed great dreams and deep ambitions of how we might somehow bring hope to people and help make society better. However, the "me generation," obsessed with materialism and motivated by greed, rubbed out the chalk marks around those fresh ideals. Our ego-centered lifestyles distort our vision so that we see a commitment to helping improve society as childish or unrealistic. Society, so the current mood goes, is not to be improved—only tolerated or drained of its pleasures.

And, what about our first real expressions of faith in God? Those were high moments in our spiritual development. It all may have started in a Sunday school class, or perhaps at the altar of the church, or in the midst of a revival meeting. We may have been young and timid and vulnerable. Maybe our profession of faith was weak and faltering. But we made it just the same and we felt we would never forget that moment. Sometimes, though, the storms of life have a way of washing off the markings we reverently put around that first encounter with him. Sometimes neglect does it. Sometimes cynicism. In any case, we realize one day that God seems so far away and we can't remember how to get back where we once began.

It's amazing, isn't it, how sometimes our experience is so similar to that of Arthur Mayer. By the way, the man who was buried was found in good condition. Maybe it's time we did some digging ourselves. It could be that those special moments in life that we thought were lost forever are, after all, still okay. Let's find out.

23

Take a Look
Inside Yourself

Scripture Reading:

Philippians 4:4–7

The famous newspaper columnist Ann Landers once wrote: "One out of four people in this country is mentally imbalanced. Think of your three closest friends—if they seem okay, then you're the one."

It's a humorous thought, but it also brings up a common problem in our day, the issue of emotional illness. According to the Reports of the President's Commission on Mental Health, in 1978 an estimated 30 million Americans were receiving some form of emotional therapy. Actually, since the early 1970s psychology has become a popular way for many Americans to deal with their problems.

In our day the stigma of seeing a psychiatrist or

psychologist is not nearly as severe as it once was. In some circles those who seek professional help with their emotional problems are considered more well adjusted than those who don't. And, they should be. After all, you couldn't be considered very bright if you knew you had something wrong with your foot and yet refused to go to a doctor. A mangled foot has a way of making you crippled if you don't get it cared for. In the same way damaged emotions don't usually heal themselves. And if they are ignored, they, too, can cripple and handicap us.

Psychology as a science and a field of medicine has changed drastically over the years. It has come a long way since the days of the phrenologist who would finger the bumps and dents in a child's skull in order to determine character and mental ability. Psychologists today use a more novel approach. They ask penetrating questions and listen. But mostly they listen.

Jesus was a master of psychology. He knew that our outward hangups are manifestations of inner conflicts. When you think about it, it was Jesus, not Freud, who originated psychoanalysis. Analyzing one's thoughts, one's hidden fears, one's honest emotions, is what Jesus did in his teaching ministry.

In spite of all the help available today, the inward look is still hard to take. But as Jesus taught us long ago, it is the step that can often lead us to peace of mind and emotional health.

24

Honesty

Is No Easy Thing

Scripture Reading:

2 Corinthians 13:5–8

Honesty really is the best policy, as the saying goes. We feel good about ourselves when we're honest. Somehow the whole world seems brighter when we struggle to be true. Even when the truth is painful.

Children, I suppose, are our greatest examples of honesty. If they don't like something, they tell you. Like the grade-school girl who was asked by her teacher to review a new book. The next day the child stood before the class and said, "This book tells more about penguins than I am interested in knowing." Polite, but to the point. One day I was trying to put together a variety of colors and designs in the clothes I was putting on. Caleb walked into the room and I asked him what he thought. With all the honesty of a six-year-old he said, "It doesn't look good, Daddy." I asked, "What's wrong?" He replied, "It's ugly." What else could be said? I put on my gray suit.

Honesty comes harder for adults. Being real is one of our greatest challenges. We try to hide our fear of failure, our insecurity, our doubts, behind such things as big bank accounts, university degrees, trophies, and fashions. Sometimes we even try to hide behind religion and God. This is a great tragedy. If faith in God means anything it means that because of it we come to face our true self. For most of us this is a frightening experience, possibly because we think we'll see things we don't like. Maybe we will. But we can never be completely authentic until we look within, and after honest investigation say, this is me, this is who I am, this is what I have to give to God. It is in this act of honest humility that we discover God's acceptance and forgiveness. Finding our own identity and our own uniqueness enables us to free the people around us in the same way. Once we accept who we are and offer ourselves to God, then we can accept others and love them with a new freedom and commitment.

Archbishop Fulton J. Sheen once wrote: "The complexities of our civilization force us to organize into larger and larger units; we have become so intent on governing what is outside of us that we neglect to govern our own selves. Yet the key to social betterment is always to be found in personal betterment."[1]

1. Fulton J. Sheen, *Way to Happiness* (New York: Garden City Books, 1954), p. 5.

Indeed, we cannot improve our behavior. We cannot adjust our character. In fact, we cannot experience conversion—until we are honest. And this is a challenge we all must take!

25

Man—

How Do You Spell It?

Scripture Reading: Genesis 1:26–31

The author of Genesis offers a poetic and mysterious account of man's origin. In the mist of Eden with the scent of fresh flowers brought by a cool breeze, we are told: "Then the Lord God took some soil from the ground and formed a man out of it; he breathed life-giving breath into his nostrils and the man began to live."[1]

There aren't many details here. A lot has been left to our imagination. But then, details were not the point. The Genesis account of creation was never intended to be a first-edition textbook on science, biology, or even history. The emphasis of Genesis is simply that God is behind creation.

1. Genesis 2:7, *The Good News Bible*—Old Testament: Copyright American Bible Society, 1976; New Testament: Copyright American Bible Society, 1966, 1971, 1976.

Now, what about man? There is a fascinating scene in Eugene O'Neill's old play, "The Great God Brown." When the main character, Brown, lies dead on the street, a policeman bends over his body and asks, "Well, what's his name?" A bystander replies, "Man." Then the policeman, with notebook and pencil in hand, turns and says, "How do you spell it?" That is a major question isn't it? How do you spell *man?*

The scientist would say man is a mixture of chemicals, atoms, and molecules. The physician would say man is made up of tissues, cells, blood, bones, and vital organs. The psychologist would tell us that man is mind, ego, personality, emotions. The minister would say man is soul and spirit.

Of course, there are some people who tell us that man is monster, a fallen creature driven by evil impulses and perverted drives. The idea is that man is basically selfish and full of the devil. There are others, though, who maintain an opposite view. They define man almost as a god. He is the "captain of his fate, the master of his soul." Whatever evil he does is chalked up to immaturity, ignorance, or a certain quirk of nature.

The truth is that man does not fit either of these extremes. He is somewhere between them. Perhaps Dostoyevsky, the brilliant Russian writer, was right when he said man is neither good or bad, moral or immoral, but rather a combination of powers and passions and possibilities, both angelic and diabolic.

What makes the difference, however, is that we believe what the author of Genesis recorded: "And God said, Let us make man in our image, after our likeness. . . ." This is our heritage. The divine image in us may be marred but it is not lost. We are all God's created children, and it is this realization that challenges man to live responsibly.

26

A Brave,
Upstanding Tree

Scripture Reading: Psalm 18:1–6

The trees in front of our Information Center looked dead. The office staff was concerned. We felt sure the harsh winter weather in January had fatally wounded the trees. The leaves on them were brown and brittle like old newspaper. Spring was in the air but it seemed to have no effect on our trees. The grass was greening. Flowers were beginning to bloom. We could see tiny buds in the other trees around the church. But those in front of our office were still withered, and dry, and lifeless. A couple of experts were called in to give their advice. They studied the trees carefully. Each branch was examined. The experts looked solemn. One shook his head in a gesture of hopelessness. The prognosis? We would have to wait. It was too soon to tell.

We waited. Some of us, I think, gave up. We forgot about the trees. Then, it happened. Someone in the office asked if I had noticed the trees in front. "I think they're budding," was the comment. And they were!

Today the trees look good. They are filling out with healthy green leaves. Some of the older brown leaves still remain, kind of like scars, reminding us of the cruel winter weather the trees had endured.

When I look out the office window and see those two trees struggling to be healthy and strong, I'm reminded of Ralph Spaulding Cushman's poem:

> I love a tree,
> A brave, upstanding tree!
> When I am wearied in the strife,
> Beaten by storms and bruised by life.
> I look up at a tree, and it refreshes me.
> If it can keep its head held high,
> And look the storms straight in the eye,
> Ready to stand, ready to die,
> Then by the grace of God can I—
> At least with Heaven's help, I'll try;
> I love a tree, for it refreshes me!
>
> I love a tree!
> When it seems dead,
> Its leaves all shorn and bared its head,
> When winter flings its cold and snow,
> It stands there undismayed by woe;
> It stands there waiting for the spring—
> A tree is such a believing thing.
> I love a tree,
> For it refreshes me![1]

1. V. Raymond Edman, *The Disciplines of Life* (Minneapolis: World Wide Publications, 1948), p. 136.

The two trees in front of our office are a picture of us, aren't they? Life has its storms. We know what it's like to be in winter. We've felt like spring inside, too. Living and dying and living again. That's what it's all about. And in the changing seasons of our life, God is with us.

Today, look up at the trees and smile and whisper a prayer. You'll be refreshed.

27

What in the World

Is Prayer, Anyway?

Scripture Reading:

Ephesians 6:17–20

I don't know about you, but I often find prayer a difficult experience to understand. And yet, the Bible is filled not only with examples of people praying, but it also has admonitions galore that we who follow Christ should pray.

Beyond that, we all have within us the need for prayer. There are times when every human being needs and wants to be in contact with God, or at least with some power greater than one's own self. Even Auguste Comte, the famous French philosopher, who admitted he didn't believe in God, the soul, or immortality, nevertheless instructed his students to spend two hours a day in prayer. He did this because he said this "act" was one of the primary functions of human nature.

In his book, *The Paradox of Happiness*, Paul Elbin has provided helpful insights into the meaning of prayer. He quotes a line from an old hymn which reads: "Prayer is the soul's sincere desire, unuttered or expressed. . . . " Then he comments:

> In this simple sentence James Montgomery stated a profound truth: Prayer is "felt," and it may or may not be spoken . . .
>
> The husband who mumbles, "How could I have spoken so harshly to the woman I love?" is praying a prayer of bitter repentance.
>
> The teacher who looks over a classroom filled with young life and muses, "I must try harder to understand them," is deep in prayer.
>
> The father who watches his little daughter at play and resolves with grim determination, "By God, no harm will come to her," is praying earnestly, not swearing.
>
> The surgeon who leaves a party early the night before an operation and goes to bed sober for the sake of another human being is living a life of prayer.
>
> The executive prays sincerely when he says, "This is a hard decision. But I have to live with my conscience, and only one right decision is possible."
>
> . . . . Prayer is man's secret weapon in his lifelong warfare with worry, fear, boredom, unhappiness, cowardice, temptation, evil, betrayal, disease, and finally death. But the purpose of prayer in the arsenal of man is not to change God. It is to change man.[1]

1. Paul Nowell Elbin, *The Paradox of Happiness* (New York: Hawthorn Books, Inc., 1975), pp. 59–60.

All of this reminds us that prayer can't be completely defined or put into a set formula. There isn't just one way to do it. You can pray anywhere, any way, any time. What is important is that we take time often to express to God our deepest inner needs and wants. When we do this, we pray.

28

The Necessity of Hope

Scripture Reading: Titus 2:13–15

Hope. It's essential to life. We cannot live without it. Pliny, the ancient Roman scholar was right, "Hope is the pillar that holds up the world."

I remember reading of that day when the gifted athlete, Florence Chadwick, failed to finish her swim across the English Channel. She quit within just a few yards of the shore. When reporters asked why she gave up, she blamed the heavy morning fog. Then she said, "If I could have seen the shore, I would have made it." Limited vision caused her to lose hope. It can happen to all of us.

The news these days is not very encouraging. Violence in the streets. War abroad. An unpredictable economy. The continued threat of some nuclear holocaust. The crumbling of traditional moral foundations. Teenage drug addiction. Teenage pregnancy. Teenage suicide (now the highest ever).

Then there's still the ever growing problems of divorce, abortion, and alcoholism. These are the kinds of realities that can, if we're not careful, blur our vision of hope and cause us to despair, give up, and quit.

Hardly anyone believes in the basic goodness of man anymore, and this is a great tragedy. It's true we hear of his many hideous and cruel acts. But man is still capable of much good and demonstrates it every day. We just don't hear about it. Goodness is not as sensational as evil. For some odd reason, we'd rather hear about some weirdo who cut off his dog's leg and fed it to his mother-in-law than we would the news that our local library received a new micro-film machine. And yet, it doesn't take a genius to see which of these events offers hope and which doesn't.

You see, hope is the result of what we believe—about God, about others, about ourselves. I find it interesting that most of the builders of Europe's medieval cathedrals were men who could not read, or write, or multiply. And yet, look what they produced. One of the professors at Princeton has referred to those men as the greatest artistic engineers of all time. How did they do it? Someone believed in them. Someone said, "I have great hope in you." And up went some gorgeous, majestic cathedral.

The ministry of Jesus was characterized by hope. He believed in people. He convinced a thieving little tax collector that he could be more; he could be honest. Jesus put hope into the lives of countless others. Why shouldn't we?

Fosdick once prayed: "Today put Christ in our

remembrance and those strong and radiant lives who have followed in his steps. Awaken gratitude in the hearts of some of us who have forgotten to give thanks, and around the evil that depresses us throw great memories and wide hopes." Let this be your prayer, too.

29

Go Where There Is No Path

Scripture Reading: Psalm 16

Following and leading. Isn't that what life is really all about? Aren't most of our days spent in following some path set before us by parents, friends, colleagues, Hollywood advertisers, and others? So much of the time we don't even think about where we're going. Like those worn-out old horses you can rent at riding stables, we just amble along some beaten-down path day after day, head down and eyes forward, hardly aware of anything else around us.

It's true that some old paths are worth following because they take us to the experiences of others that have been rewarding and worthwhile. But life can't be all following. Someone has to lead, and that opportunity is open to virtually all of us.

In his book, *From the Land and Back,* Curtis K.

Stadtfeld offers some interesting insights into this business of path-making. He writes:

> Students wear paths across the campuses of universities, beating down the grass, defying all barriers, ignoring all sidewalks. Student paths have two things in common: they are invariably the shortest distance between two points, and they are straight.
>
> Cow paths are neither. They always wander and turn a little, and never go straight to the object.
>
> Humans take the straight route, intent not on the journey but on the destination. We largely miss the trip, thinking ahead to a future time.
>
> Cows do not think ahead, and perhaps see more of the countryside. Their paths are unhurried, and more fun."[1]

Hurrying through life taking short cuts and missing all the scenery is common practice in our day. It's not, however, creating the kind of paths anyone in upcoming generations will want to follow.

What is needed today are folks young and old who will take time to observe and study life, and be both follower and leader. Follow the paths that lead one to faith, to joy, to service. And establish paths that open new ways to these same experiences.

An old proverb says, "Do not follow where the path may lead. Go, instead where there is no path and leave a trail." This is a challenge we all can take. The psalmist said, "God will show me the

---

1. Quoted in, "Points to Ponder," *Reader's Digest*, 118:32 (September 1980).

path of life."[2] Indeed he will. And it is in following him that we learn how to get off the beaten trail occasionally, and set off on some new adventure of faith, and life, and hope, leaving behind us a path for others to follow.

2. Psalm 16:11.

30

You Can Begin Again

Scripture Reading:

Matthew 28:1–8

I'm sitting here in my office looking at a jar full of candy Easter eggs. What possible significance could these little purple, and yellow, and pink eggs have? Not much. They're fun to hide. They're kinda tasty. They're cute. But that's about it.

What *is* significant is a wooden cross and an empty rock tomb. Easter eggs have a way of going out of style. Nobody is passing them around on the Fourth of July. The cross and the empty tomb, however, are always with us. The crucifixion of Christ and his resurrection have significance no matter what time of the year it is.

In Arthur Miller's fascinating play, *After the Fall*, the main character, a fellow named Quentin, sits and talks to God. Quentin is feeling desperate. He is being honest. He is struggling to make sense out of his life. He's convinced, though, that he is losing the struggle. Nothing seems to add up. He feels he hasn't been anywhere in life and he isn't heading anywhere either. He describes his situation in these dramatic words:

> . . .despair can be a way of life; but you have to believe in it, pick it up, take it to heart, and move on again. Instead, I seem to be hung up. And the days and the months and now the years are draining away. A couple of weeks ago I suddenly became aware of a strange fact. With all this darkness, the truth is that every morning when I awake, I'm full of hope! With everything I know—I open my eyes, I'm like a boy! For an instant there's some—unformed promise in the air. I jump out of bed, I shave, I can't wait to finish breakfast—and then, it seeps in my room, my life and its pointlessness. And I thought—if I could corner that hope, find what it consists of and either kill it for a lie, or really make it mine. . . .[1]

All of us, in some degree, eventually find ourselves in the place of Quentin. We, too, have to choose between despair and hope.

The message God has given us at Easter is that wherever you are in life He is with you, and whenever you face the despair of crucifixion, be ready also for the hope of resurrection.

In other words, new beginnings are always possible. If life has crucified you—if you have crucified

---

1. Arthur Miller, *After the Fall* (New York: The Viking Press, A Bantam Book, 1964), p. 5.

yourself—don't despair. God offers resurrection. With him, you can start over. With him you can corner that hope. You can make it yours. And nothing is more significant in life than that!

31

What Are the Things
that Matter?

Scripture Reading: Luke 19:1–10

Winston Churchill once told of a sailor who jumped into a river to save the life of a little boy. Several days later, the sailor met the little boy and his mother as they were walking down the street. The mother stopped, and said, "Are you the man who pulled my son out of the water?" Expecting some word of gratitude, the sailor said, "Yes, ma'am." And the mother replied, "Well, then, where's his cap?!"

This incident makes us wonder what really matters in life. Aren't we too often taken up with things that are trivial, unimportant, insignificant? Like the woman who turned down the chance to take an afternoon foliage tour with her church group because she didn't want to miss her soap opera. Or like the business man who missed his daughter's graduation because he had promised to attend a golf tournament with an important client.

All of us are guilty of this sort of thing. We, too, have exchanged memorable experiences for passing flings. We have traded once-in-a-lifetime moments for everyday happenings and routine encounters.

Suppose Zaccheus had decided to stay home and polish his sandals, or had gone to the bank to count his money, instead of climbing a sycamore tree to watch for Jesus? Sure, it was a daring thing to do, and people thought it strange that he sat in that tree, but there was adventure and a sense of expectancy in what Zaccheus did. Catching a glimpse of the Christ was more important than anything else for that little tax collector. For once he had his priorities in place.

What really matters in life? Caps? Soap operas? Golf tournaments? Polished sandals? Not really. How about love? Well, yes, that matters. Caring for family, friends, people, that adds meaning to life. A warm embrace, a tender "I love you," a thoughtful act—these things matter.

How about God? Yes, he too matters. Receiving his grace, accepting his forgiveness, living in his presence—this is important for all of us. Life is a puzzle with missing pieces without him.

How about church? It also matters. Joining together in worship, singing our faith, stretching our soul and mind in Bible study—this is so vital.

Jesus warned us in his Sermon on the Mount not to throw our pearls in the pig trough. I think that meant, be sure to know what really matters in life!

32

The Wilderness
Within Us

Scripture Reading:

Ephesians 2:11–13

Those who have no personal relationship with God must find life somewhat perplexing, perhaps even meaningless. Immanuel Kant's three great questions of philosophy—What can I know? What ought I to do? What can I hope?—have no answer if God is not personal, if He is not interested in me and my world.

Not long ago I was reading the opening verses of Genesis. The creation account is a wonderful piece of literature. It is full of mystery, and miracle, and marvel. But those first few verses give us a kind of picture of man without God. We are told that the earth was without form, that it was void, and that darkness was everywhere. Then God "moved upon" this vacant mass and his creative powers produced all kinds of wonders. The result was life.

How similar life without God is to the shapeless, empty earth that rested in darkness. This must have been a desolate place before God's creative influence was ever felt. And so it is with us before we come to know this great God. H. A. Williams comes close to describing the situation in these words:

> . . .the wilderness belongs to us. It is always lurking somewhere as part of our existence, and there are times when it seems pretty near the whole of it. . . . Most people's wilderness is inside them, not outside. . . . Our wilderness, then, is an inner isolation. It's an absence of contact. It's a sense of being alone—boringly alone, or saddeningly alone, or terrifyingly alone. Often we try to relieve it—understandably enough, God knows—by chatter, or gin, or religion, or sex, or possibly a combination of all four. The trouble is that these . . . can work their magic only for a very limited time, leaving us after one short hour or two exactly where we were before."[1]

There really is a barrenness, a desolation, even a wilderness within us before we come to realize that God can be met, felt, experienced, believed. And even after we meet him in faith it never completely goes away. There's always something of the wilderness in us. We're always unfinished, undeveloped, weedy in some areas. But His creative presence does have its influence. Our personal relationship with him in faith allows us to blossom, to flourish, to be fruitful. He gives us, not new life, but simply more of

1. H. A. Williams, *The True Wilderness* (New York: The Crossroad Publishing Company, 1982), pp. 29–30.

life itself. And we understand that it is his presence with us that gives our existence meaning.

We don't have to go looking for God. He's always with us, always has been. He didn't stumble onto the formless mass of earth. He'd been there, before it, all along. He's always waiting to create. He has something in mind for you. Take a risk. Exercise some faith. Welcome him. And remember these words, "And God saw every thing that he had made, and, behold, it was very good."[2]

2. Genesis 1:31.

33

The Automatic Out

Scripture Reading: 1 Peter 1:13–21

Duty. Responsibility. Accountability. Not very popular words in our day, are they? Our generation likes to talk about "freedom," and "doing your own thing."

Gregg Easterbrook, a contributing editor to *The Washington Monthly,* published an editorial in which he said, "More and more people are ordering their lives along a principle I call the 'automatic out.' " He explained what that means. Folks today want a stopping place in their love affairs, their community relationships, and their jobs in order to avoid the "troublesome" aspects of life. They don't want to make any kind of commitment that is going to require or demand something from them. What they're looking for is a situation that will give them something.

This is a very shallow, selfish approach to life, and it may well be the basis of all evil. If there's one thing the world needs forgiveness for and re-demption from, it's this attitude of taking without giving, expecting something for nothing, draining others of everything dear to them and then drop-ping them like a disposable Coke can.

We see so much of this in society today. And to an extent, we're all guilty of living by the "automatic out." If we are not getting from our marriage what we think we deserve, we terminate it. We have children for the sheer pleasure they bring us, but then conven-iently ignore them when their stages of development demand too much of our time and energy. We attend Sunday morning church for the "lift" it gives us, but somehow can't find the time or interest to get in-volved in the other services or the rest of the church activities and programs. When called on to help carry some of the load, we promptly offer our excuses and mutter something about not feeling qualified, as if there were some sort of unattainable requirement for Christian service.

Plato once said the excess of liberty soon be-comes the excess of slavery. I think what he meant was, if all we're interested in is the freedom to do what pleases us, then we eventually become the slave of our own selfishness. This is what happened to King Solomon, and his conclusion on life was, "all is vanity." Or we find what one greedy, self-absorbed man discovered—"You reach the end of the rainbow, and there's no pot of gold. You get your castle in Spain, and there's no plumbing."

Perhaps Ignatius, Bishop of ancient Antioch, had the right idea when he prayed: "Teach us, good Lord, to serve thee as thou deservest; to give and not to count the cost; to fight and not to heed the

102

wounds; to toil and not to seek for rest; to labour and not to ask for any reward, save that of knowing that we do thy will; through Jesus Christ our Lord." It is with this kind of commitment to God, to life, to others, that we learn to say no to the principle of the "automatic out."

34

Is There a Way
Out of Trouble?

Scripture Reading:

Matthew 6:25–33

In his intriguing story, "The Housebreaker of Shady Hill," John Cheever confronts the reader with a disturbing paradox. The principal character in the book is a fellow named Johnny Hake. He is one of the residents of a wealthy, cultured neighborhood. He lives around people who are world travelers, who enjoy good music, and who may choose a book by some ancient Greek philosopher or perhaps a Catholic theologian if they were buying a paperback in an airport gift shop.

Hake is a civilized, respectable man-about-town. Then comes the paradox. Because of financial problems of huge proportions Hake resorts to common thievery. And yet it's not so common after all. This

104

troubled, well-to-do man begins a career of robbing the homes of his affluent friends late at night. Johnny Hake maintains his high standing in the community by paying his bills with money he has secretly stolen in the night from his neighbors.

The paradox, however, becomes too overwhelming. He cannot live this schizophrenic lie. It is at last the force of a reality outside himself, in the form of a sudden rain shower, that restores his sense of values and opens up his spiritual life. He explains this mystical experience in the following words:

> I wish I could say that a kindly lion had set me straight, or an innocent child, or the strains of distant music from some church, but it was no more than the rain on my head—the smell of it flying up to my nose—that showed me the extent of my freedom . . . . There were ways out of my trouble if I cared to make use of them. I was not trapped.[1]

What a beautiful and extraordinary example of Christian truth. To be sure, few of us will be shaken from our sins by an unexpected cloudburst, but anything that will convince us we are not trapped in our personal conflicts, that there are ways out of our trouble, is without a doubt the work of God.

Someone reading this may be wrestling with his or her own enormous paradox: How to be loving when you feel bitterness and hatred. How to be caring and thoughtful when you want so much for yourself. How to be forgiving when you are full of

1. John Cheever, *The Stories of John Cheever* (New York: Ballantine Books, 1980), pp. 318–319.

personal pain. How to have faith when you are consumed by doubt. How to be strong when you know so well your weaknesses.

These are some of the dilemmas we all face eventually. But like Johnny Hake we can discover we are not trapped in life. There are ways out of our trouble if we care to make use of them. Our Christian faith can show us how to begin.

35

The Power that Makes Us Strong

Scripture Reading: Luke 17:20–21

The Swiss have an athletic event they call "Unspunnen." It has been a favorite game among farmers and herdsmen in that country since the fourteenth century. The contest consists of—are you ready for this—each participant heaving a 185-pound rock as far as he can. The world record, set in 1980, is a whopping 3.7 yards.

As you might guess, this sport has a limited number of contestants. The average person is not equipped for this grueling test of strength. Only the very powerful can play.

Two thousand years ago the disciples of Jesus had their own test of strength. Their leader and teacher had announced that he would die. The kingdom of God, he declared, would not come about through brute force. There would be no clashing of swords between the Christians led by Christ and the Roman army led by the emperor. Jesus would not come into the holy city riding a great white horse. He would, instead, ride down the streets of Jerusalem on the back of the humblest animal around, a common donkey. There would be no royal crown, only a plain and rugged cross. No glorious takeover, but rather, a humiliating death.

When the disciples heard that, they must have felt as weak as kittens. They truly believed that Jesus would soon be the next king of Jerusalem, Rome, and the rest of the known world. Now he was talking about dying, and with that his followers began to realize that all their dreams would soon be nailed to a wooden cross and destroyed on a hill outside Jerusalem.

What would they do? Where would they go? How would they survive? They had serious questions, and Jesus gave them a compelling answer. "In the world ye shall have tribulation," he said, "but be of good cheer; I have overcome the world."[1]

Overcome is a big word. It is a word of power. In the language of Jesus it meant, "to carry off the victory." What victory? Jesus had in mind the disciples' victory over fear, pride, selfishness, jealousy, prejudice, bitterness, hypocrisy, and all those other destructive emotions that make life so narrow that they squeeze out all our joy and love and faith and hope.

Jesus said one day that the kingdom of God is

1. John 16:33.

108

within us. The disciples finally realized, after his death, what Jesus meant by that. We must learn the meaning of it too.

Committing your life to Christ and receiving his Spirit is the way to begin. And in time, we discover from following our Lord, a strange and wonderful inner power, not a power that corrupts and makes us rigid, and judgmental, and pious. Rather, it is a power that enables us to "overcome" those emotions that rob life of its meaning. It's the kind of power that makes us strong, even stronger than Swiss herdsmen who've been known to throw huge rocks almost four yards!

36

Exposing Faith
to Life

Scripture Reading: Habakkuk 2:4;

Romans 1:16–17

George H. Morrison, the great Scottish preacher, once told his Sunday morning congregation: "You will never know how strong the lighthouse is, till it has stood the buffet of the storm. You will never be certain that the bridge is stable, till it has borne the weight of heavy loads. You will never fathom the dignity of man, till you have seen him tried and tested by alternatives."[1]

Here is great preaching, for in these words we are reminded of a fundamental truth in religion, that our faith is worthless unless it is exposed to life's choices.

---

1. George H. Morrison, *The Footsteps of the Flock* (Grand Rapids: Baker Book House, 1977), p. 10.

Too many times we want our Christian experience to shelter us from the tough issues of everyday living. We want Christ to protect us and shield us from pride and lust and selfishness. We'd like to think that our faith is a kind of invisible wall around us keeping back all the evils of our world.

All of us are, as George Morrison said, "tried and tested by alternatives." We are confronted daily with choices and our faith helps us make our decisions. Will we be honest in our business or go for the shady deal? Will we remain faithful to our marriage partner or give in to selfish desires? Will we hold a grudge or be forgiving? Will we try to be sensitive to others or keep on doing things our way? Will we complain about how bad things are or will we try to find some good somewhere? Will we give in to despair or hold on to our hope? God doesn't protect us from these crucial decisions. They are a part of life. No one can decide for us. We have to face these issues on our own. Our faith, of course, gives us direction. Like a good map it shows us the most sensible roads to take. But the final travel plans are up to us. We have to choose where we're going and how we'll get there.

That's why some people are disappointed with the Christian experience. They thought it would be different. They supposed life would be easier, more simple, that the tough issues would somehow be settled. They discovered, however, that all the old temptations are still there. The old friends, too. And in some instances, the old habits. "Doesn't God take all this from us?" they thought. No, He doesn't. We have to choose. That's why we need our faith, and his presence.

111

The alternatives of life will always be with us. But then, so will he. And when it comes time to make our choices, as difficult as they sometimes are, at least we'll know we're not alone.

37

Watch Where You Look!

Scripture Reading: Luke 10:21–24

A good many years ago the famous French general, Charles DeGaulle, visited the United States. He stayed in New York City and while he was there he was taken to the top of the tall RCA building. It was a beautiful day and the view was clear for fifty miles in every direction. The General observed the scene with interest. One of his companions asked him what he thought of the breathtaking view. General DeGaulle paused and then asked, "Where's Coney Island?"

The great French leader did something we're all guilty of. He looked for the wrong thing. He was seventy stories above ground looking at some of the most fascinating sights in America. He could have spotted the Statue of Liberty or the Brooklyn Bridge or West Point, all national historic landmarks. But instead, he strained his eyes to see Coney Island, a crowded and littered amusement park.

It's easy in our day to miss the vision of beauty and grandeur and see only the common, little ordinary things that don't amount to much. I guess it all boils down to what we're looking for.

If we adopt the philosophy of our day then our view becomes merely a narrow focus. We, too, seem to be looking for fun, pleasure, amusement. There's nothing wrong with any of that except when those experiences become the only thing in view.

The Bible is full of examples of folks who lost sight of what was important because they were looking in the wrong direction. Solomon is a case in point. For a time he glittered with bigness but he turned out to be a very small man. Considered one of the greatest kings of Israel he lifted his kingdom high only to let it fall in shame and disgrace. Builder of the great temple, husband of a thousand wives, leader of a mighty army, this man with so much potential went looking for the wrong things. This servant of God who prayed for wisdom and an understanding heart restricted his view to the insignificant and fleeting pleasures of his day. He lost sight of the desperate needs of his people. He no longer saw the pain and hunger and injustice around him. His eyes were fixed on cedar palaces and fast horses and golden drinking cups. As his view narrowed, so did his heart and soul. And the result? He wasted a great inheritance and left a kingdom broken, rebellious, and overwhelmed with discontent. This brilliant leader with such high ideals and noble dreams for God and his people became a selfish tyrant. He died in scorn and scandal and disrespect. His concluding philosophy was, "Life is useless."

114

Such is the fate of all who miss the greater vision of service, compassion, and love, and look only for those experiences in life that offer cheap thrills and momentary pleasures. How about you? Are you looking for national landmarks or just another old amusement park?

38

Living for the
Right Reasons

Scripture Reading: James 4:13–17

What is the meaning of this great mystery we call life? Just thinking about it fills me with wonder, and joy, and a sense of adventure.

A Catholic priest has made some insightful comments about this business of living. He writes:

What is life? That mysterious thing which is so intimately bound up with my thoughts, my ambitions, my pleasures, and my destiny; Life—that which at times thrills me and at times saddens me; Life—that which sometimes seems the greatest of all my gifts and at others the most burdensome of all; Life—that which ushers itself in with a cry and takes its leave with a moan; Life—that which I know best and which I know least—what is it?[1]

1. Fulton J. Sheen.

116

Do you ever get the feeling today, as I often do, that a great many folks are somehow missing the meaning of life? At times I even find myself in that crowd. We shuffle through our days following some ordinary routine until, to our amazement, the days have become years and we approach death wondering what happened to life. Where did it go? How could it have passed so quickly? The children are grown. Your best friends have died. Retirement is "old hat." Your health is fading. Tomorrow seems so uncertain.

Could it be that we become so involved in preparing for life that we fail to live it? Or is it possible that we live for all the wrong reasons?

Mozart, the brilliant Austrian composer, wrote more than 600 pieces of music. But in his day he was hardly recognized. He never received a prize, honor, or award for his music while he was living. He died so poor that he was buried in a common grave with ten others. But today, he is one of the best-loved composers in music history. In Salzburg, Austria, his name and picture are on everything. Mozart is known and loved throughout the entire world.

His life was his music—not fame, or wealth, or success, or those other things that you and I so often associate with meaningful living. We really do live for the wrong reasons sometimes, don't we? In our frantic quest for success or whatever, we miss the flowers, the children, the sky, the music, and all those things that make the journey from birth to death so worthwhile.

Henry Van Dyke once said, "Be glad of life because it gives you the chance to love and to work and to play and to look up at the stars." So it does. We all look forward to heaven, but how tragic it would be to wake up someday and realize that we had gained heaven but had missed life. Perhaps this is why God will wipe away the tears from some of us when we get there. Because you see, missing life will really be something to cry about.